STORIES OF PIONEER LIFE

FOR YOUNG READERS

BY
FLORENCE BASS

Purple House Press
Kentucky

TO

My Father and Mother

WHOSE MANY STORIES OF EARLY TIMES HAVE ALWAYS
AROUSED MY CHILDISH AS WELL AS MY MATURE INTEREST

THIS BOOK IS AFFECTIONATELY INSCRIBED

Published by
Purple House Press
PO Box 787
Cynthiana, Kentucky 41031

Classic Books for Kids and Young Adults
purplehousepress.com

Copyright © 2025 by Purple House Press
Written by Florence Bass in 1900
Cover: Currier & Ives, 1867, after Frances Flora Bond Palmer
The Pioneer's Home on the Western Frontier
Yale University Art Gallery

Unabridged
All rights reserved

ISBN 9798888181416

Contents

	To the Children	v
I.	OUR LAND—PRESENT AND PAST.	1
	Introduction. Indian children. Indian women. Indian men. Hunting.	
II.	THE COMING OF THE WHITE MAN.	11
	Indians and the white man. Indians and guns. Indians and horses. Change in the Indians.	
III.	MARQUETTE, MISSIONARY.	17
	Preparing for the journey. Among the strange Indians. Down the Mississippi River. Marquette's last trip.	
IV.	HUNTERS.	24
	Camps. Weapons. Game.	
V.	DANIEL BOONE.	28
	First visit to Kentucky. Attempt to remove his family. Building the fort. Capture of the children. Finding the children. Boone's capture. His escape. His later days.	
VI.	FLAT-BOATS.	39
	An old man's story. Another Indian story.	
VII.	BLOCKHOUSES AND FORTS.	43
	A pioneer's story.	

Contents

VIII.	DOWN THE OHIO—MARIETTA.	45
	The second *Mayflower*. Mounds in Ohio. The new home. Story of Isaac Williams. Story of Lockhart. Story of Josiah Hunt. Story of Captain Wells. Peace with the Indians.	
IX.	STORY OF FRANCES SLOCUM.	58
	The lost girl. Her life among the Indians. Her discovery.	
X.	ABRAHAM LINCOLN.	67
	His first home. His life in Kentucky. Removal to Indiana. A new home. A better home. Lincoln at school. Lincoln a young man.	
XI.	AN OLD SETTLER'S STORY.	77
	Lost in the woods.	
XII.	A STORY OF EARLY TIMES.	81
	Leaving the old home. Indians. The winter. The founding of Indianapolis.	
XIII.	GRANDFATHER'S STORY.	88
	The trip down the river. The journey to the new home. Food. Clearing land and raising corn. After the harvest. Schools. Clothing. Lack of conveniences. Money. Pioneer preachers. Mails. Difficulties of trade. Roads. New settlers. Stages. Cars. Telegraph.	

TO THE CHILDREN

Dear Little Friends:

Here is a book of stories about real people and what actually happened not so very long ago. Indeed, many people are still living who saw things like these of which I tell you.

I hope that these stories will help you to look with respect upon aged people. Even if they have not had such trials as I have described, their lives have in some way helped to make your life pleasant.

You know that Longfellow says:—

> "Lives of great men all remind us
> We can make our lives sublime,
> And, departing, leave behind us
> Footprints on the sands of time."

This does not mean only those great men whom all the world knows. There have been many great men and women whose names even are not known. They have just as truly left their "footprints on the sands of time" as if we could tell who they were.

Look at this beautiful country of ours, with its rich farms, its good roads, and its fine cities and towns with their pleasant homes. Think of its safety from Indians and wild beasts, of its many churches and schools, and of its bright flag of freedom. All these are the footprints of the brave pioneers who lived before us.

I am sure that such things make us feel as if we should like to live noble lives, and leave worthy footprints to guide those who follow us.

Your sincere friend,
Florence Bass, 1900.

I. Our Land—Present and Past.

I. INTRODUCTION.

Boys and girls, do you not often ride through the country on the cars? You like to go gliding along many miles in a few minutes!

WAVING AT THE TRAIN.

It is pleasant to look out from the car window at the beautiful fields, meadows, and woods! You like to watch the horses, sheep, and cows run away as the train goes rushing by!

Sometimes children come out of the farm-houses and wave at the cars. You are sorry for them because they are not riding on the cars, also!

When the train stops at the little towns and the large noisy cities, you enjoy watching the people, who get on and off the train. You wonder where they live and where they are going.

I am sure that our country seems very beautiful and interesting to you. Did you ever think that it did not always look as it does now? Less than one hundred fifty years ago the central part of it was a wilderness.

INDIAN BABY.

No one could have seen the country then from a car window. There were no cars, no railroads, no good roads of any kind. There were no farms, no towns, no houses even, such as we now see. No white people lived in this region.

There were great forests, beautiful rivers, and wide prairies. There were many wild animals, such as deer, bears, and buffaloes. Here, too, lived the Indians, who were almost as wild as the animals.

II. INDIAN CHILDREN.

If we could have gone into the forest then, we might have found other babies in the trees besides those of the squirrels and birds. Often an Indian baby in his queer cradle would swing from the branch of a tree. His cradle was a board covered with skins, dried moss, or grass. Till he was two years old, the Indian baby spent most of his time tied to this board.

He was carried about on his mother's back or hung up away from harm as she worked. It was of no use for him to cry. The first lesson that he had to learn was to bear discomfort. He learned this lesson well, for after a while he would bear any pain without a cry. He would go hungry for days without complaining.

His first plaything was a bow and arrow, with which he soon learned to shoot well. It was a proud day for the Indian boy when he was able to kill a deer.

INDIAN BOW AND ARROWS.

He learned to fish and to swim while he was only a tiny boy. And so he grew up, learning to hunt, to fight, and to fear no pain or danger.

The little Indian girls learned different lessons. As soon as they were able to walk, they began to help their mothers in their work.

III. INDIAN WOMEN.

Instead of the pleasant towns which we see now, there were then only Indian villages. In place of the good houses that men now build, were wigwams, or tents, made by the Indian women. They set a number of long poles in the ground in a circle and made them meet at the top. These were covered with skins, or rushes, or the bark of trees.

In the centre of the wigwam a little pit was dug for a fire. A hole was left at the top for the smoke to go out. Of course, much of it stayed inside and made the wigwam a smoky, unpleasant place.

There were no tables, beds, or chairs, and no floor but the bare earth. Skins of animals served for seats or beds.

INDIAN WOMEN AT WORK.

The Indians did not stay in their wigwams as we do in our houses. They lived out of doors most of the time. The forest was their home.

Often a whole Indian village would be moved. Then the Indian women pulled up the wigwams, carried the poles and covering to the new camping place, and set them up again.

The Indian woman planted and tended the little patches of beans, corn, and melons. Of course she did all the cooking. She knew how to bake before the fire a rough kind of cornbread, and how to cook corn and beans.

She could make soup in a wooden kettle. She did this by

CARRYING THE WIGWAM.

heating stones very hot and dropping them into the soup. When these were cool, they were taken out and more hot ones put in. This was done over and over till the meat and soup were cooked. Besides all this the Indian woman had to prepare the skins of animals for clothing and then make the clothing.

Do you not think that she had much hard work to do? Yet she did not wish the Indian man to help her. She thought such work not fit for him.

IV. INDIAN MEN.

INDIAN WARRIORS.

Such men as these lived in our country in the early times. How different they look from the men we see here now!

Think of the work that you see men doing now,—farming, building, buying and selling, making beautiful and useful things of all kinds. The Indians cared for none of these. Their chief delight was to fight. They were often bitter enemies to Indians of another tribe, and fought very cruelly. When an Indian killed an enemy, he took his scalp. This means that he cut off a little piece of the skin with the hair just at the crown of his head.

The Indian that had taken the most scalps was thought to be the bravest of all. Sometimes Indians took their enemies captive and treated them very cruelly. But a brave Indian would show no sign of pain.

INDIAN PEACE-PIPE.

When Indians made peace with their enemies, they smoked the peace-pipe together. Offering the peace-pipe was always a sign of friendship.

Sometimes Indians who had gone to war wished to send a message to their friends very quickly. We might think that they had a queer way of telegraphing. They found a high place that could be seen far away, and here they built a little fire of something that made a big smoke.

One column of smoke meant the success of a war party. Little columns near by told how many scalps were taken. Sometimes the fire was smothered and then allowed to go up in puffs. In that way some other message was sent.

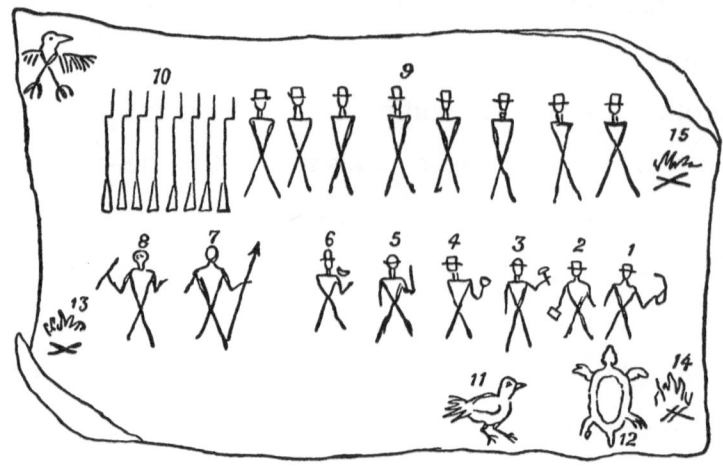

INDIAN LETTER ON BIRCH BARK.

Once an Indian wrote a letter like this. It was written on birch bark and stuck into a pole which was set slanting in the ground. The pole pointed in the direction in which the party had gone. Three notches were cut in it to show that the party would travel for three days.

The letter itself tells of their three camp-fires of the night before, and of the prairie hen and turtle that they had cooked. The men without hats are Indian guides, and the others are white men.

Would not that seem to us a queer way to write a letter? Sometimes such writing was put upon rocks or skins of animals. An Indian wrote a kind of history in this way. A picture was made to show something that happened each year.

I am sure that we should not like such books and letters so well as we do our own.

V. HUNTING.

Indians spent much time in fishing and hunting. They did not hunt for sport, but because they needed the animals for food and their skins for clothing. It was sometimes hard to secure the game, for before the white man came the Indians had only clubs and bows and arrows to use in hunting.

In winter the Indian sometimes wore snow-shoes when he went hunting. These held him up on the soft snow so that he could run many miles in a day. He could easily bring down a deer, for it could not run so fast, as its feet sank into the snow.

When the Indians could not catch game or fish, there were often days when they had very little to eat. They did not know how to keep food, and to provide for all times, as we do.

You see why the Indians roamed about. They could not always find game in one place. They must go where it could be found.

INDIAN WEAPONS.

No one Indian owned a certain amount of the land as your fathers do. A great part of the country belonged to a tribe of Indians, and they roamed over it as they pleased. No one could buy or sell any of it, but all might hunt or camp on it.

Some parts of the country seemed to belong to no one tribe. As many different tribes hunted there, bloody battles were often fought.

You can see why the Indians did not want the white man to come into this country to live.

The white man took the land for his own. The game was soon killed off, and the Indian lost his hunting ground.

INDIAN WITH SNOW-SHOES.

II. The Coming of the White Man.

I. INDIANS AND THE WHITE MAN.

Do you wonder how the Indians felt when they first saw white men? Here is a story telling of some Indians who had never before seen or heard of a white man.

Several Indians were one day going through the woods, when they came to some trees that were cut in a strange way. At first they thought it must be the work of beavers, but they saw that this could not be so, for the chips were too large.

A beaver could not open his mouth wide enough to cut such big chips. At last they said, "Some great under-water animal must have done it."

They saw a place where a tree trunk had been cut down and dragged away. They followed this path or trail, and soon found footprints of an animal. The footprints did not seem to them like those of men, for there was a deep place at the heel. The Indians did not know that these prints had been made by shoes with heels, for they had never heard of such things.

Soon they looked through the brush and saw the animals at work. At first the Indians thought that they were bears, but as they came a little nearer, they thought that perhaps the workers might be men. Yet they had hairy faces—a great deal of hair hanging down from their chins.

The Indians hid behind the trees and watched them. Some of the white men were piling up logs while others were picking up sticks.

"SOME GREAT UNDER-WATER ANIMAL MUST HAVE DONE IT".

The Indians were afraid to come nearer. One of the oldest of them said: "Perhaps they will smell us or feel us here. Perhaps they will kill us. Let us go away." So they went back to their camp.

They said: "We saw some queer water animals that looked much like people. They had white faces with much hair on them. Some had red bodies and some were black."

The Indians did not know that it was the men's clothing that was red and black.

AN OLD-FASHIONED GUN.

II. INDIANS AND GUNS.

Many Indians were then eager to see these strange animals. So they went carefully through the woods and found them still at work. One Indian said: "I will go first alone. If they try to hurt me, you must all rush out and we will fight them."

Soon the Indian came up to one of the white men, who looked straight into his face and stretched out his arm. The Indian did not know that he wanted to shake hands.

Then more of the white-faced creatures came up and the Indian saw that they were men. The white people made motions for the Indians to come into their house; but the Indians did not understand, or were afraid to go.

At last, some of them dared to follow the white men. When they came back they told the others what strange things they had seen. A white man showed them a queer-looking stick. He poured some black sand into his hand and then into a hole in this stick. He took a round thing out of a bag and put this also into the stick.

The Indians watched him very closely. The white man began to make strange signs to the Indians; but they did not understand. He made a loud noise with his mouth and pointed to the stick.

He put his finger on the under part of it and motioned for the Indians to do the same. One of the Indians did so and there was a terrible crash.

The Indians were very much frightened for they had never seen or heard a gun before. They were not long in learning the power of this queer stick.

The white men showed them their knives and axes, and how to use them. The Indians were surprised to see how quickly a white man cut a log in two with a big axe. They wanted guns, knives, and axes themselves. They soon found that the white men would give them these things in exchange for skins of animals.

KNIVES AND AXES.

III. INDIANS AND HORSES.

Once a man was in camp near an unfriendly tribe of Indians. He had not been able to kill any game for some time, and so he had no food. At last he decided to ride into the Indians' camp and offer to exchange his horse for food.

This tribe of Indians had never seen horses. As the man came riding in, an old chief said: "Here is something very

The Coming of the White Man

strange. I have heard of many wonderful things; but I have never heard of anything like this. This thing must have come from the sun or out of the earth. Do not say anything to it. Be still and wait. If we try to hurt it, perhaps it will go into that hill again."

At first the Indians were very much frightened, but as it came nearer they saw that it was a man riding a strange animal.

The man patted the horse's neck, and made signs to show that he was friendly. At last he made the Indians understand that he had been without food for a long time, and would give them the horse for some buffalo meat. Then they gladly gave him food in exchange for his horse.

When the Indians first got horses, they did not know what to feed them. They would offer them pieces of dried meat. The horses would turn away, put down their heads and eat grass.

RIDING TO THE INDIANS' CAMP.

Very soon the Indians began to have horses of their own. One Indian owned so many that he was named "Many Horses."

IV. CHANGE IN THE INDIANS.

It is easy to see how the Indian changed after white men came. He soon got guns and knives and horses from them. Then he could kill game more easily and travel much faster and farther.

The white men gave him another thing of which I am sorry to tell you. That was rum. The Indian called it "fire water," which is a good name for it. He soon became very fond of it. He would give almost anything for the "fire water" of the white man. Yet what a wicked and cruel man it made of him!

When white men first came over the sea into our country, most of the Indians were friendly with them. They thought that the white men came from the sky.

It is hard to tell whether Indians or white men did the first wrong; but it is certain that in many places they both did very many cruel things.

The Indians captured or killed the white people in the most dreadful way. They soon began to think all white people were their enemies, as they came farther and farther into the country and drove the red men from their hunting ground.

III. Marquette, Missionary.

I. PREPARING FOR THE JOURNEY.

I AM SURE that all boys and girls know what a missionary is. You know that he goes to teach people about the Bible, and how to live better lives. You have often given your pennies to help send a missionary to some far-off country. You think of those countries as far away in another part of the world.

STATUE OF MARQUETTE.

Would it not seem strange to think of missionaries coming to our own beautiful country? Yet missionaries were among the very first white people to come into the middle part of the United States.

Marquette was a good missionary, who left his pleasant home in France and came here over two hundred years ago. The white people had heard of a great river in this part of the country, and a man named Joliet was sent to find it. Marquette came with him to teach the Indians about God.

These two men chose five other Frenchmen to come with them. They built two small canoes of birch bark, into which they put plenty of smoked meat and Indian corn.

BIRCH-BARK CANOES.

Marquette had already been teaching the Indians for two years, and had learned to speak their language. The Indians had tried to keep him from going away into unknown lands. They said that the river was full of great monsters that would swallow his boats. They told him that the heat down the river was terrible, and that the Indians were unfriendly and would kill him. But Marquette said that he was willing to lose his life for a chance to teach the Indians.

II. AMONG THE STRANGE INDIANS.

Marquette and Joliet with their five friends started out on Lake Michigan in their two little boats. They went down into Green Bay, then into the Fox River. From here they carried their boats a mile and a half across the land to the Wisconsin River.

They sailed down this unknown stream to find the great river of which they had heard. At night they camped on shore. They roasted their meat before the fire, and slept on skins and blankets.

ON LAKE MICHIGAN.

In about a month they were made happy by the sight of a great river which they were sure must be the Mississippi that they had started to find. Here they saw huge fish that made them think of the monsters of which the Indians had told them.

Now they began to fear savage Indians, so they did not land at night, but slept in their boats in the middle of the river, one man keeping watch while the rest slept.

For two weeks they saw no Indians. One day they saw footprints in the sand and a path leading from them. Joliet and Marquette followed the path till they found an Indian village. Soon the Indians crowded out to see them. They offered the white men the peace-pipe to smoke, which showed that they meant to be friendly.

The Indians told them that their visit made the sun more bright, the sky more blue, and the earth more beautiful. Was not that a pleasant way to say that they were welcome? Marquette told the red men of the God who made them and that they should obey Him.

Afterward the Indians gave Marquette and his men a great feast. An Indian fed them as if they were children, putting the food into their mouths. Next morning several hundred of these red men went out with them to their boats.

They gave the missionaries a peace-pipe and bade them a friendly good-by.

III. DOWN THE MISSISSIPPI RIVER.

On and on down the great river these tiny canoes floated. By and by the explorers came to the place where the Missouri River rushes into the Mississippi. Its strong current almost upset their boats. Still they went bravely forward. The weather became very warm, and the mosquitoes tormented them night and day.

At one place many savages rushed out with a war-whoop to attack them. Some even aimed their bows and arrows at the white men. One Indian threw his war club at them.

At last the older men of the village came out, and kept the young warriors from hurting the white men. The Indians saw the peace-pipe which Marquette held up, and invited him to land with his followers. This they did with great fear, but they were feasted and well-treated. Marquette tried to teach his hosts the truths of his religion.

The Indians warned the white men not to go farther down the river, for fear of the savage tribes there, so Marquette and Joliet decided to return at once.

What a hard trip it was, going back up the river against its strong current! Marquette became very weak and ill, and suffered much.

They did not return just as they went, but rowed up the Illinois River. From here they carried their boats across the land to the Chicago River, and so sailed into Lake Michigan.

CARRYING THE BOATS.

It is believed that the great missionary Marquette once visited the spot where Chicago now is. From here they paddled up to Green Bay, the place from which they had started. They had been gone four months, and had travelled over twenty-five hundred miles.

IV. MARQUETTE'S LAST TRIP.

Marquette was very anxious to get well so that he might go back and preach to the Illinois Indians, but it was a whole year before he was able to start.

He took two Frenchmen and a number of Indians with him. He had ten canoes this time. They went down Lake Michigan to the Chicago River.

The weather was cold and stormy, and Marquette became ill again. They went about five miles up the river and built a rude hut. Perhaps this was the first house built by white men where the great city of Chicago now stands.

Marquette spent the cold, dreary winter here, but in the spring he grew somewhat better. So he went on to preach to the Illinois Indians. As he went from wigwam to wigwam, he was received with great joy.

At one time he preached to a great council. Five hundred chiefs were seated in a ring, behind whom were fifteen hundred young men and warriors, and back of these were all the women and children of the village.

These people begged Marquette to stay and teach them, but he knew that his life was nearly over, so he started back to his old mission at Mackinac, where he had first taught the Indians. His friends rowed him carefully up the river as he lay weak and ill in the boat.

They crossed Lake Michigan, but he felt that he could go no farther, so he asked his friends to land. They built him a bark hut, and cared for him as tenderly as they could.

It was not long before he died in this little hut in the wilderness. He was glad to give his life in trying to do good to the Indians.

IV. Hunters.

I.

WHEN WHITE PEOPLE first came to this country, it was not to make their homes here. Some came to find out what kind of country it was. Some of them came to teach the Indians about God. Others came to trade with the Indians or to hunt.

Hunting was not a day's sport with such men; it was the work of a season. In the fall they hunted the deer. The winter and early spring was the time to hunt bears and other fur-bearing animals.

A HUNTER'S CAMP.

Hunters

Sometimes hunters built a camp like this. Often a hunter had no shelter in which to sleep. Then he would roll himself up in a buffalo skin, and lie on the ground with his feet toward the fire.

The hunter had a queer kind of clothing well-suited to the woods. Over one ear hung the bushy tail of a raccoon, for his cap was generally made of that animal's skin. He wore a long coat and leggings made of fringed deerskin, and had also deerskin moccasins. Such clothing could not be easily torn, and would not wear out very soon.

The hunter always carried with him his trusty rifle. His well-filled powder-horn was swung over his shoulder. He had also an Indian tomahawk which he used in clearing a way through the forest. He carried a long, keen-edged hunting-knife to be used in taking the skin from any animal that he might shoot.

A HUNTER WITH HIS WEAPONS.

With his knife he cut off bits of meat which he placed upon a forked stick and roasted before the fire. Often his meat was eaten without salt. Perhaps this was the only kind of food that he had for months.

When the hunter killed a buffalo, he was supplied with both food and bedding. The animal's shaggy skin made a fine warm blanket for him.

BUFFALOES ON THE PLAIN.

II.

These hunters were brave, strong men. They had to protect themselves from wild animals and Indians, and to provide their own food and clothing.

They knew well how to use their rifles. They could load very quickly and fire very accurately They thought it was a disgrace to waste a shot. Their aim was so sure that one man would even hold a board between his knees as a mark for another to fire at.

A hunter stood with his back against a tree when loading, that he might not be surprised by an enemy.

Once a hunter, who was able to load while running, was pursued by Indians. He fired his gun, killing one of them. The rest thought he could not shoot again, so they dropped their guns that they might run faster. But the hunter loaded as he ran. Soon he turned and fired again. He did this two or three times. At last the Indians gave up the chase, saying, "No catch dat man; he gun always loaded."

V. Daniel Boone.

I. FIRST VISIT TO KENTUCKY.

Daniel Boone was a great hunter. He had heard of the beautiful country of Kentucky, which was beyond the mountains west of his old home.

Boone and five other hunters came over the mountains into this beautiful land. It was a fine hunting ground with many deer, bears, wolves, panthers, buffaloes, and other animals.

DANIEL BOONE.

For six months the hunters roamed through the forests. One day in the winter Boone and another man were captured by the Indians.

For a long time they saw no chance of escape. In order that the Indians might not watch them so closely, they acted as if they were satisfied to stay.

One night they found a chance to slip away without being seen. How glad they were to be free from the Indians again! They went back to the camp where they had been with the other hunters, but alas! no one was to be seen! Boone and his friend did not know what had become of their companions.

One day Boone's brother and another man came over the mountains to join them. Boone must have been delighted to hear from his home! There were now four white men in the forest together. But the cruel Indians were watching them; and it was not long before they killed two of the hunters, and only Boone and his brother were left.

Soon the brother went home for more powder and lead, leaving Boone alone in the great forest. He must have felt strange with no friend near. He had not even a horse or a dog for company. His only food was the game that he killed; he had no bread, salt, or sugar.

CANE BRAKE.

To hide from the Indians he often slept in the cane brakes, where all night he could hear the howling of wolves. There were about him many kinds of fierce, wild animals, and at all times he was in danger from the Indians

But Boone was not afraid, for he loved the beautiful forest in spite of all its dangers. After three months his brother came back with powder, lead, and other supplies.

II. ATTEMPT TO REMOVE HIS FAMILY.

Boone wandered through the forests of Kentucky for nearly two years; then he went back to bring his family into the forest to live.

It was some time before they were ready to go. Several other families started with them to make their home in the new country.

At night they camped out in rude tents which were made of poles and covered with bedding. Day and night the people were on the watch for Indians.

One day the men who drove the cattle had dropped somewhat behind the others, as the cattle could not go so fast as the people did. Suddenly a report was heard from the guns of the Indians who had been hiding behind trees. Six men who drove the cattle were killed. One of them was Boone's son.

How sad all the people were then! They would go no farther into the new country so full of Indians. They went back to their old homes beyond the mountains.

III. BUILDING THE FORT.

You may be sure that Boone was not willing to leave this beautiful land to the Indians. He wished to make a home here himself.

Some time after this he and several other men came again. They cut down trees and built a strong fort.

There was a two-story log house at each corner of the fort. There were loopholes in the upper part through which the men might shoot. Such houses were called blockhouses.

There were also several smaller cabins. The spaces between the cabins were filled by a high log fence, which was sometimes

DANIEL BOONE'S FORT.

called a stockade. The logs were sharpened at the top and set deep in the ground, close enough to touch each other. Heavy wooden gates were made, to let the people in and out of the fort.

When this fort was done, Boone went back for his wife and children. This time they reached their new home in safety. The horses and cattle were driven into a large open space in the centre of the fort. Before long several families were living here.

IV. CAPTURE OF THE CHILDREN.

As long as the people stayed in the fort, they were not in much danger. The Indians could not get in, and their bullets could not go through the thick walls. But the men needed to go outside to fish and hunt.

The women, too, knew how to use rifles, and they would shoot an Indian if he tried to harm them when the men were away. They could kill a deer if one happened to come near.

The men must go outside the fort to plant and tend their little crops of corn, beans, and potatoes. The Indians did not trouble this fort very much for some time, so perhaps the people grew a little careless.

One day three girls went outside the fort. One of them was Boone's daughter Jemima, who was about fourteen years old. The other two were Betsey and Frances Calloway, fourteen and sixteen years old.

They saw a boat on the river and said, "Let's have a little row." So they got into the boat and splashed merrily about for some time.

At last they turned to go home, when suddenly two fierce-looking Indians sprang out of the woods and seized the boat. Three more appeared, ready to shoot the girls if they tried to get away. They screamed loudly, and Betsey fought with her oar, but it did no good: the Indians carried them off through the woods.

Betsey reached up and broke the bushes as she passed along. She knew that her father would look for her, and she hoped he might follow her by seeing the broken bushes. The Indians soon made her stop this. Then she tore off little bits of her dress, and dropped them by the way.

The girls were much frightened to be carried thus away from home! They did not know how the Indians might treat them.

V. FINDING THE CHILDREN.

You may believe there was trouble in the fort that night. When the hunters came home, they were told that their daughters had been carried away by the Indians.

Boone with several others started out at once to hunt for them. They went very carefully, for they thought, "If the Indians see us coming for the girls, they will kill us and escape."

All the next day they kept up their search. Often they were guided by a broken bush or a bit of Betsey's dress. At last they saw a light smoke curling up through the woods. They peered through the bushes, and there with the Indians were their daughters, nearly worn out with terror and fatigue.

Just as the hunters were ready to fire, the Indians saw them and ran, but not without losing four of their number.

The girls were now safe from their terrible danger. They had feared that they should never see their homes or parents again. They had been taken thirty miles from the fort. The journey back seemed much shorter. No words can tell how great was their joy at being free from the Indians.

VI. BOONE'S CAPTURE.

One thing that the people needed very much in the fort was salt. Not far away were some springs where the water that came up was very salty. Such places were called salt-licks, because many animals used to come here to lick the ground about the spring, for animals, too, need salt.

A salt-lick was a good place to go hunting. The men could hide in the bushes near it, and when the animals came, it was easy to shoot them.

Men also came here to get salt for themselves. They boiled the salt water a long time. At last the water would disappear, and leave the salt.

One day Boone and some other hunters went to a salt-lick to make salt. Suddenly a number of Indians rushed out, captured Boone, and carried him away many miles.

The Indians watched him very closely. They did not intend to let him escape this time. As before, he acted as if he were willing to stay with them.

ANIMALS AT A SALT-LICK.

They soon grew very fond of him. An Indian adopted him in place of a son that he had lost. His head was shaved like an Indian's, and his face was painted until he looked like one.

Sometimes they let him go out to hunt. They made him show game for every bullet they gave him.

But he was sharper than they were. He cut the bullets in two, and saved half for himself. He was getting ready to run away.

VII. HIS ESCAPE.

Boone stayed with the Indians a long time, for he found no chance to escape. The people at the fort thought that he was dead, and his wife went back to her old home.

One day he heard the Indians planning to go to his home, break down the fort, and kill the settlers. He knew then that he must escape to save his people.

The next morning he started out to hunt. He managed to slip away without being seen. He knew that the Indians would surely kill him if they found him again.

He dared not fire a gun, fearing that the Indians might hear it and find him. He could not light a fire, for fear they might see the tell-tale smoke.

For four days he travelled almost without stopping. During that time he had but one meal, which was a little dried meat he had carried with him.

On the fifth day he came in sight of the fort. He seemed more nearly dead than alive, having travelled one hundred sixty miles almost without food or rest. How surprised his friends were to see him!

He told them of the Indians' plans against them. They made ready for the attack, and when the Indians came some time later, they were not able to break down the fort. It was saved because Boone had been so strong and brave.

VIII. HIS LATER DAYS.

As the years went by, many more white people came to live in the new country. They were able to do some farming. Boone himself became a farmer as well as a hunter.

One day he was at work in his drying shed, hanging up tobacco to dry. Four strong Indians slipped quietly in at the door before Boone saw them. Pointing their guns at him they said: "Now, Boone, we got you; you no get away any more. We carry you off this time, sure. You no cheat us any more, Boone."

Boone looked down in surprise. He soon saw that they were the Indians whom he knew when he was a captive before. It seemed as if he would have no chance to get away this time.

BOONE'S TOBACCO-DRYING SHED.

He must have thought pretty fast as to how he could escape. He did not seem to be at all alarmed, but spoke to the Indians as friends. He kept talking to them pleasantly while he went on with his work.

He gathered up a few handfuls of very dry tobacco and suddenly threw the dust into their faces and eyes. Then he jumped down, pushed them aside, and ran past them very quickly.

They could not see him, for they were blinded by the fine tobacco dust. They stamped and raged with pain and anger at the trick he had played them. Boone was soon in his cabin and able to defend himself.

He lived to be a very old man, but he was never again captured by the Indians.

VI. Flat-boats.

I.

YOU REMEMBER that Boone and his friends journeyed across the mountains into the new country.

Many other people came down the Ohio River—not in steamers of course, for there were no such things in those days.

A FLAT-BOAT.

They came in a flat-boat or house-boat. Sometimes it was called a "Kentucky Ark." It was a large flat raft, with a tent or little house upon it.

Here one or two families lived as they floated down the river. Would it not seem strange to camp out on a boat?

Such a boat could not go very fast, for it simply drifted down the river. The oars were used only to guide the boat. It was not always easy to make it go where the men wished. Sometimes it stuck fast upon a sand bar, and then it was hard work to push it into the water again.

Of course people did not travel very fast in flat-boats; but they were not in a hurry in those days. Sometimes it took several weeks to make the trip down the river.

In the early times such a journey was full of danger. The Indians were always watching for white people, and they were ready to capture and kill all they could.

Hundreds of these boats drifted down the river in the early times, and hundreds of people were killed by the Indians. Do you not think travellers must have been very brave to face such danger?

II. AN OLD MAN'S STORY.

Here is a story, told by an old man, of what happened when he was a little boy.

"When I was ten years old, I came with my father's family down the Ohio River in a flat-boat. Several families were in one boat, and our cattle were in another.

"We were gliding down the river very safely, we thought. About ten o'clock at night we heard the terrible yells of the Indians who had a number of fires along the shores. As they kept this up, we thought that perhaps they had captured some white men and were killing them.

"We fastened our two boats together, and floated on as quietly as possible, hoping that the Indians would not see us.

"Just as we came opposite their fires, they commanded us to 'come to.'

"We were perfectly silent, for father had given strict orders that not a sound should be made, except from a gun. About a hundred Indians with a fearful cry jumped into their canoes and followed us. On we floated in dead silence; not an oar was touched.

"They came within a few yards of us. My mother quietly put an axe by the side of each man, keeping a hatchet for herself. The Indians kept on yelling and following us for three miles; still not a word from us! not a sound!

"At last the Indians became awed by this strange stillness. Perhaps they thought us a boat full of dead men floating down the river. They ceased to follow us, and we were safe once more."

III. ANOTHER INDIAN STORY.

People who were attacked by the Indians did not often escape unharmed. Once a party of men, women, and children were coming down the river in a flat-boat.

Just at daylight, one foggy morning, some one called to them from the shore, asking to be taken on the boat. They knew that this was only a trick of the Indians to get them near the shore. The men at once left their oars and went to their guns. The women and children were told to lie flat on their faces on the cabin floor and to keep as still as death.

Before long several canoes full of painted savages came swiftly toward them. Tables, boxes, and chairs were thrown from the flat-boat, that there might be more room to fight. The Indians were soon at hand; and a close, hot fight followed.

Three of the white men were killed and others were badly hurt. Several Indians lost their lives, and at last the rest pushed off for the shore, fairly beaten.

None of the women or children was hurt, except one little boy. When the fight was over, he asked to have a bullet taken from his scalp.

"That is not all, captain," said the brave little fellow, as he held up his arm, showing where it had been shot at the elbow.

"Why did you not tell us of this before?" asked his mother.

"Because the captain told us to be still," said the little boy. He was surely a brave little lad to bear so much pain in silence!

VII. Blockhouses and Forts.

I HAVE TOLD you about the fort in which Boone and his friends lived, and how it was made to protect them from the Indians.

In those days all new settlers had to live in or near a fort. If there were only a few families, they sometimes had only one blockhouse. Their own little farms and cabins were not far away. Here they lived except in times of danger.

Sometimes they would hear that Indians were near, or a report would come that some one had been killed by them. Then every white person would hurry in great fright to the blockhouse.

One pioneer tells us what he remembers of such times:—

A BLOCKHOUSE.

"When I was a little boy, the fort to which my father belonged was three-quarters of a mile away from our farm. Sometimes we were waked up in the dead of night, on account of danger from the Indians.

"Once a messenger came softly to the house and gently tapped on the door, telling us that the Indians were near. Every one of us was up and wide awake at once. Father seized his gun, while mother dressed the children as quickly as she could.

"I was the oldest of the children, so I was able to help carry things to the fort. There was no chance to get a horse to take us there, so we walked and carried what clothing and food we could find in the dark. We dared not light a candle or even stir a fire, fearing that the Indians might see us.

"We were as quiet as possible, as we made ready to leave our home. We took great care not to wake the youngest child, lest he might make a noise. The one word 'Indians' was enough to keep the rest of us still. In a short time we were all safe inside the fort."

Often a number of families would be in their own home in the evening, and before morning they would all be in the fort. The next day men with loaded guns would go back to the cabins and bring such needed things as they had not been able to take the night before.

The families stayed in the fort until the danger seemed past. Then they went back to their little cabins again.

VIII. Down the Ohio—Marietta.

I. THE SECOND *MAYFLOWER*.

You have heard of a great war in this country which made us free from English rule. You have been told what a hard time our soldiers had and how bravely they fought.

When the war was over, there was not money enough to pay the soldiers, so our government offered to give them land in the new country, north of the Ohio River. There they could make new homes for themselves.

A number of them decided to go, and they began at once to make ready for the long journey. One cold day in December they left their homes in the East, starting out for the "Far West," as they called it.

They followed the Indian path over the mountains. After eight weeks they reached a small river. They expected to go the rest of the way to their new homes by water.

It was now so cold that they could go no farther till spring. While here, they built a large, strong boat which they named the *Mayflower*. Probably they were thinking of the little ship, *Mayflower*, that brought the Pilgrims to America many years before this.

This boat was not much like the ship for which it was named. It had a roof and strong sides that could stand against the bullets of the Indians.

In April all the little company entered this rude boat and floated down the river. On and on they went, down into the beautiful Ohio.

They landed opposite Fort Harmar, which was held by a number of soldiers. This fort made the people feel somewhat safer from the Indians.

How pleased they were with the new country that they had reached! Such big, fine trees they had never seen. Such rich, black soil and such fine weather were very promising. They began at once to build their houses. While building, they lived in the *Mayflower*.

There were fewer than fifty people in this first company. In about three months they were joined by nearly a hundred others, who had travelled nine weeks to reach this new home.

II. MOUNDS IN OHIO.

In this new country there were some queer earth mounds which were a great wonder to the new settlers. They were somewhat like little hills; but they were perfect in shape, smooth and regular. You know real hills are seldom like that.

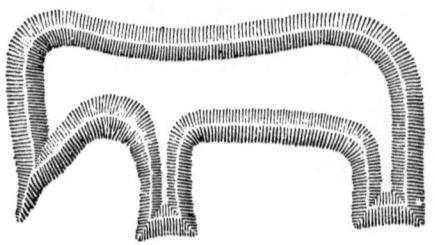

ELEPHANT MOUND.

Some of these mounds were built in the shape of animals. One was like an elephant, and another was like a serpent. The mounds were made so long ago that great trees have had time to grow upon them.

The Indians who lived there could not tell who built the mounds. Men have never found out surely who made them.

We know only that these mounds were made by men far back in the past, so it will hardly do to call this a new country. Indeed, it must be a very old country, though it was new to the people who came here a little over a hundred years ago.

The new settlers wished to preserve these old mounds. They built a fort upon one of them, thinking they could not find a better place. They took such good care that the mounds should not be destroyed that very many of them are still to be seen.

MOUNDS NEAR MARIETTA.

III. THE NEW HOME.

The fort which the settlers built was white-washed and looked very fine as the sun shone on it. They dug a well inside the fort, then began to clear the land and plant corn.

They laid out a little town, which was called Marietta. Then they made laws for their town, which were written out and nailed to a tree where everybody might learn them. All the people seemed glad to obey them.

Before long a preacher came to live among these pioneers. He preached to them on Sundays, and taught the children during the week. They had their school and their church in one of the blockhouses.

At first they were very happy in their new home. The soldiers at the fort said they had never seen such happy people.

CAMPUS MARTIUS.

The soil was so rich that the corn grew fast and tall. One man said to his friends in the East: "Why do you waste your time trying to raise corn there? Here we have to stand on tip-toe to break off the ears. There you have to stoop down to get it." Another man said, "It would be as easy to be lost in a cornfield as in a cedar swamp."

Though the settlers enjoyed their beautiful, rich country, they had their troubles, too. They could not work outside the fort without danger from the savages. They must always be protected by armed men. The Indians could not bear to see the white man's corn growing on their hunting ground.

As hundreds of white people began to settle in this new country, the Indians grew more enraged.

At last they said in anger, "No white man shall plant corn north of the Ohio River."

They did all they could to drive the white men out, killing many and carrying others away as prisoners. The Indians burned the crops and destroyed as much game as possible so that the settlers could not find food.

TALL CORN.

This soon led to war with the Indians. There were many cruel and bloody battles. At last, after a long time, the Indian was compelled to let the white man make his home in the new country. Then many of the Indians went farther west. Those who did not go were friendly to the white people.

IV. STORY OF ISAAC WILLIAMS.

Fear of the Indians was not the only trouble the early settlers had. Sometimes it was hardly possible to get food.

At one time people had to eat nettles and potato tops. Once, food was so scarce that little children had to live on half a potato a day.

NETTLE.

At another time the people had nothing fit for use in making bread. It happened in this way. They had planted their corn as usual, but before it was ripe there was a heavy frost. After the corn was gathered it became mouldy, and when it was ground and made into bread, it made many people ill.

Yet even this poor corn sold at such a high price that the settlers could hardly afford to buy it.

I fear many of them would have starved, had it not been for a kind man, whose name was Isaac Williams. He had planted his corn early, and had gathered a fine harvest before the frost.

Some men who wanted to make money tried to buy his whole crop, offering him a dollar and a quarter a bushel for it.

Isaac Williams would not sell it to them. Instead, seeing how badly the settlers needed it, he let them have it for fifty cents a bushel. If they had not the money, he gave them the corn, taking only their promise to pay when they were able.

He was willing to help his neighbors, though he lost money by it. Such men make the world better.

V. STORY OF LOCKHART.

Some time after this one of the settlers was ill. When he began to get well, he wanted some deer meat. He asked a man, named Lockhart, to go into the woods and kill a deer for him.

It was a dangerous thing to do, because there was an Indian war at the time, but Lockhart said at once that he would go. He went out into the forest and soon killed two fine deer. Then he started back for the fort.

Suddenly he met two Indians in the path. They were as much surprised as he was. Seeing his rifle, they at once sprang behind trees.

One of them happened to choose a tree too small to cover him. So Lockhart fired and wounded him.

Then the other Indian rushed out, thinking that the gun could not be fired again at once. But Lockhart had reloaded instantly and was ready for him.

The Indian, seeing that he was ready to shoot, ran back to the tree again. Lockhart, too, hid behind a tree. There both men stayed until it was nearly dark. Each was afraid to come out, be-

THE INDIAN BEHIND THE TREE.

cause that would give the other a chance for the first shot.

At last Lockhart thought of a plan to get the Indian to leave his tree. Putting his hat on the end of his ramrod, the hunter pushed it very carefully around the tree.

It looked to the Indian as if the man himself were peeping around the tree, so he fired at the hat and rushed out to get his scalp. This gave Lockhart the chance he wanted. He fired at the Indian, and killed him instantly. Then he went in safety to the fort with his deer.

VI. STORY OF JOSIAH HUNT.

Once during an Indian war there was a very brave hunter named Josiah Hunt. It was his duty to supply game for the men at the fort.

It was almost impossible to leave the fort without being shot at by the Indians. They used to climb trees near by so that they could watch any one who came out. Then they would follow, and perhaps kill him.

Hunt always left the fort at night so that he could not be seen. He said, "When I am once in the woods, I have as good a chance as the Indians." In the night he went to that part of the forest where he expected to hunt the next day.

In winter he needed a fire to keep from freezing, but he must not have any flame, or the Indians might see it. So he dug a hole in the ground about as big as the crown of a hat. This he filled with strips of white oak bark, which will burn somewhat, even if covered with ashes.

After the fire was started, he nearly covered it with earth, leaving only two or three little holes to let in the air. To keep off dampness, he spread his blanket over strips of bark. He sat upon this with the fire between his legs.

HUNTER RELOADING HIS GUN.

He always kept one hand upon his rifle, that he might be ready for the Indians at all times. In the morning he began to hunt. Very carefully he went, looking for deer and Indians.

If he saw a deer, he would put a bullet in his mouth, so that he could load again the minute after he had shot. He would reload his gun before he started to pick up the deer he had killed. He feared that the Indians might have heard him shoot, and would be ready to kill him.

When he skinned a deer, he did so with his back against a tree, and with his rifle within reach of his hand.

This hunter was so careful that the Indians were never able to catch him. Some time later, when they made peace with the white men, they asked to see Hunt. They gathered about him and said, "Great man, Captain Hunt; great warrior, good hunting man; Indian no can kill."

They told him that some of their bravest warriors had often gone out on purpose to kill him, but could never find him off his guard. The Indians admired him very much for his bravery and his cunning.

VII. STORY OF CAPTAIN WELLS.

During the war with the Indians, white men were often sent out as spies. It was their duty to watch for Indians, so that the fort should not be taken by surprise.

Captain Wells was a spy of this kind. Long before this he had been captured by the Indians and taken into one of their families, where he had lived for a long time. There he had learned their language and many of their ways, so that now he was a good spy.

He dressed as an Indian, and no one would have thought that he was a white man. One day he saw a family of Indians coming down the river in a canoe. They saw Wells and paddled toward him without fear, thinking that he was one of their own people.

He soon saw that they were the family with whom he had lived. At the same time, he saw his men behind the trees ready to shoot them.

He turned his gun toward the white men and ordered them to stop, crying out that he would shoot the first one who dared to fire.

Then he said, "Those men have fed me when hungry; they have clothed me when naked; they have cared for me when I was ill; they have treated me with as much kindness as if I had been one of their own children."

The white men put down their guns at once, and hurried to the canoe to shake hands with the trembling Indians. Wells told them that they had nothing to fear from his men. He warned his Indian father to keep out of danger; then he bade them good-by. The Indians seemed very grateful, and hurriedly paddled down the stream.

VIII. PEACE WITH THE INDIANS.

I have told you of some of the troubles the settlers had with the Indians. You have seen how unwilling the red men were to give up their hunting ground, and how very unsafe it was for white people to live here. Many of them lost their lives trying to do so, but others kept trying to make their homes here.

Again and again peace was made with the Indians, but again and again war broke out. After much fighting and suffering the Indians were obliged to let the white man live here. Many of them went farther west, where for a time they again had a large hunting ground.

INDIANS GOING WEST.

Some of them still stayed in this part of the country and became friendly to the white people. It is only within the last hundred years that the people in the Ohio Valley have felt safe from the savages.

Have you felt sorry for the Indian because he was driven from his land? Remember that he used it for little except hunting. He raised few crops, he built no cities or roads or bridges.

He did not try to make himself better or to learn better ways of living. He left the land no better for the people who lived after him.

Very few people can live, even in a rich country, unless they use the land well. The Indians would not learn from the white men how to improve their land, and so they lost it all. What we do not use we are likely to lose.

IX. Story of Frances Slocum.

I.

ABOUT ONE HUNDRED twenty years ago the white people in Pennsylvania were in great danger from the Indians. There was then a family named Slocum living in that part of the country. There were several children, one of whom was named Frances.

One day when Frances was about five years old the Indians suddenly appeared near her home, and before any one knew of their approach they killed a boy near the house.

All the Slocum family were greatly frightened, and tried to escape to the woods. Mary, one of the larger girls, caught up her two-year-old brother Joseph, and ran away. Mrs. Slocum and several of the children also reached the thick bushes.

Little Frances tried to hide under the stairs, but an Indian saw her and seized her and also her little lame brother.

Then the mother rushed out and begged for her children, but the Indian only laughed at her. Pointing to the boy's feet she said, "He is lame; he can do thee no good."

Then the Indian let the lame child go, but he threw Frances across his shoulder and dashed off into the bushes.

"HE THREW FRANCES ACROSS HIS SHOULDER."

As she disappeared from sight, she put back her tangled curls with one hand, and stretching out the other toward her mother, she cried bitterly and begged to be saved.

The family searched for her in every direction. They offered much money for any news of the little girl. They did everything that they could to find her, but there was no trace of her.

How the poor mother grieved for the little child! She could not forget the tearful face as she last saw it vanishing into the woods. Over and over again she would say: "What has become of the dear child? How will the Indians treat her?"

Little Frances had had a new pair of shoes before she was taken from home. She had been required to lay them aside, to save them for cold weather. The poor mother kept thinking, "Oh, if Frances only had her shoes! How will she endure the cold in the forest with bare feet!"

The winter dragged on and no word came from the little one. Years passed, and still there was no news of the captive.

II.

Mrs. Slocum could not forget her lost child. She was sure Frances must still be alive. She could not give up the hope of finding her.

One day a woman came to the house of Mrs. Slocum. She said she had been taken captive when a child, but had forgotten her own name as well as her father's, and she had come to see if she were not the lost Frances.

Mrs. Slocum soon saw that the stranger was not her child. Still she said, "Stay with me as long as thee likes; perhaps some one will extend the same kindness to my dear Frances." The stranger stayed a few months and then went away. She felt that these were not her own people.

After Frances had been gone twenty-nine years her mother died. Even to the day of her death she believed that her lost child lived, although she had never heard one word from her.

She had told her sons never to cease looking for their sister. The brothers made many long and dangerous journeys, and spent thousands of dollars searching for her; but the time went by and they could not find her.

III.

At last nearly sixty years had gone since Frances was stolen. At this time there was a man living in Indiana named Mr. Ewing, who was an Indian trader and knew the language of the Indians.

One night he stopped at an Indian cabin and asked to spend the night. He was kindly received and well treated by an old Indian woman.

He saw that this woman did not look like most Indian women. Her hair seemed unlike an Indian's, and seeing her bare arm, he noticed that the skin was white. At last he asked her if she were not a white woman.

At first she seemed unwilling to tell him; but finally she said she was not an Indian. She told him that she had been captured when she was a little girl. She thought her father's name was Slocum, but she could not remember her own name. She could not speak a word of English.

The Indians had taken her as their own child, had reared her as an Indian, and taught her to fear white people. Indeed, she had never told her story before, fearing that the white people might come and take her away. She had married an Indian, and had at this time two grown daughters. The Indians had always treated her well, and she had been very happy with them.

Mr. Ewing thought a great deal about her story, and wondered if her family were still living. He wrote a long letter to a postmaster in Pennsylvania, telling him all that he could about the aged captive.

The letter was finally printed in a newspaper. A friend of the Slocum family saw it, and sent a copy of it to Joseph Slocum, who was then an old man. It was he who had been carried into the woods by his sister Mary at the time Frances was stolen.

IV.

What must have been the feelings of the brothers and sisters in reading of the long-lost Frances! So many times they had tried to find their sister, and failed. Surely now they would see her.

They decided to go to Indiana at once, though they were all old people, and it would be a long, hard journey. They must go through forests and over rough roads, where houses were few and far apart, yet they were willing to endure any hardship to find their sister.

Soon Joseph Slocum started and was joined by his sister Mary who lived in Ohio. Later, his brother also joined them. After several weeks they reached the Indian village where Frances lived.

How eager they were to see her! "Will she look at all like the curly-headed Frances of so long ago?" "Will she be glad to see us?" they asked each other.

Mary said, "I shall know her, if she is my sister. She has lost the nail from one forefinger. You remember, brother, that you pounded it off in the blacksmith shop about a year before we lost her?"

When they entered her house, they found her sitting quietly in a chair. At first she seemed to them very cold and distant. Of course, she could not understand a word that they said. Neither could they understand her.

They had brought a white man with them who could speak the Indian language, and could tell each of them what the others said.

At first the Indian sister even seemed to suspect her visitors of having some plan to rob her. Her brothers walked the floor in grief. Her sister wept bitterly, but Frances sat unmoved. Could it be that this was the dear little Frances, lost so long ago? How could she possibly have become this old Indian woman?

FRANCES SLOCUM.

Still there could be no doubt about it. There was the same hurt finger. She remembered her father's name, and could tell just where she hid when the Indians came to the house.

She was told that this was her sister, who ran away with the little brother, and here was the little brother, too.

Slowly she began to understand that these were really her people. She grew interested, and was willing to tell them about herself.

She told them that the Indians had painted her skin, and that they had dressed her in wampum beads which she thought very fine.

They had always been kind to her. Even now they treated her like a queen, gladly doing whatever she wished. She was quite rich, too, for an Indian.

V.

The brother and sister wished very much that Frances would go back to the old home with them. She said: "No, I cannot; I have always lived with the Indians; they have always treated me kindly. I am used to them. Why should I go to be like a fish out of water?"

Then they begged her to visit them. But she said: "I cannot, I cannot. I am an old tree. I cannot move about. I shall not be happy with my white relatives. I am glad to see them, but I cannot go, I cannot go; I have done."

Her daughters agreed with her. One of them said, "The fish dies quickly out of the water." The other said, "The deer cannot live out of the forest."

And so the brothers and sister had to return home without her, but they had much to console them. Their sister was like a queen among the Indians. Her life was not one of hardship or suffering. She had always been well-treated and was satisfied with her home.

VI.

Two or three years later Joseph Slocum visited his sister again. This time his two daughters were with him. Mr. Slocum told Frances he had brought his children to see her. All her coldness of the first visit seemed gone, and she showed great joy at seeing her brother again.

She was much pleased that her nieces had come so far to see her. She showed that she was very grateful for their visit. She offered her brother half her land if he would come and live with her. But there seemed to be no way by which the long-parted brother and sister could remain together. They parted in the most friendly manner.

The father and daughters had journeyed about two thousand miles before they reached their own home. They had been gone seven weeks and had spent nearly four hundred dollars.

As the years passed by the Indians were required by the government to leave their old homes and go farther west; but Frances and her family were allowed to remain.

She was very sad after many of her Indian friends had gone, so she asked one of her brothers to allow his son to come and live with her. This was the child that he had hoped to have near him in his old age, but he cheerfully gave him up to his poor Indian sister.

The young man came with his family and lived near his aunt, till her death. He preached among the Indians and did them much good.

Frances Slocum died when she was about seventy-four years old. She was buried in Indiana where she had lived so many years.

Now a small monument marks her grave.

X. Abraham Lincoln.

I. HIS FIRST HOME.

AFTER BOONE'S FIRST visit to Kentucky, he had so much to say about the beautiful country that many of his friends wished to go there to live. Among these was a man named Abraham Lincoln. He brought his family and made his home among the savages in this region.

One day he was out working upon his land. His little six-year-old son Thomas was with him.

Suddenly there came a shot from an unseen Indian's rifle. Mr. Lincoln fell dead beside his little boy. The Indian was about to kill the child, too, but just then he himself was shot down by Thomas's older brother.

There were five little children in the Lincoln family, left now with only their mother to care for them. Little Thomas himself soon had to make his own living. He had to go from place to place as a laboring boy.

He had no chance to go to school, and when he became a man, he could neither read nor write. When he was twenty-eight years old, he was married to Nancy Hanks. She taught him to write his name.

This rude cabin was their home, and also the first home of their little boy, who was named Abraham for his grandfather.

It is this Abraham Lincoln of whose life as a little boy I wish to tell you. He became such a great man that I am sure you have often heard of him.

II. HIS LIFE IN KENTUCKY.

You would hardly think a great man ever lived in such a house as this. See its rude stick-chimney, its rough walls and roof! The inside was just as poor. It had no floor but the bare earth. There were only slab stools instead of chairs. A broad open fireplace served to cook the food and to warm the room.

LINCOLN'S FIRST HOME.

Abraham lived here several years. He and his sister went to school four miles away. They had to walk all this distance, and carry their dinner of cold corn-bread. Their only book was a spelling-book.

Little Abe, as he was called, was very quick in his studies, and soon learned to read and write.

How hungry he was for books and stories! He read everything he could get, which was not much. He had no lamp, nor even a candle, by which to study at night. He used to get spice-wood brush and burn it, so that he might see to read. His mother could read, and very likely she told him all the stories she knew, over and over again.

III. REMOVAL TO INDIANA.

When Abraham was seven years old, his father decided to move to Indiana. He sold his little home, or rather traded it for goods. Mr. Lincoln put these goods on a raft and started down the river with them.

As he was not able to manage his raft, it was upset, and his goods were thrown into the river. He saved some of them, and these he left with a settler.

Then he walked on through a forest, to select a place for a home. He soon found a place he liked. So he went back to Kentucky for his wife and children.

He borrowed two horses, loaded all his goods upon them, and started on foot with his family. They did not have much, perhaps only a very little clothing and bedding and a few things to cook with.

Can you think what such a journey as this would be? Think of walking for miles through the strange forest! It must have been full of delight to the little children. Perhaps it was not so pleasant to the grown people. They could kill a deer, or turkey, or other wild game for food, when they wished. At night they camped out in the woods.

By and by they crossed the Ohio River into Indiana. There they hired a wagon and went on toward their new home. There was no way open through these thick woods, so that often Mr. Lincoln had to cut down trees, or trim away the brush to make a road for his wagon.

At last they reached the place Mr. Lincoln had chosen. Little Abe, though only seven years old, was given an axe, and told to help with the new house. At first they did not build even as good a house as the cabin they had left.

They built what was called a "half-faced camp" which was something like a shed made of poles. It was left open on one side and there was no floor. The fire was built outside, opposite the opening. In this poor home the Lincoln family lived for a year.

HALF-FACED CAMP.

IV. A NEW HOME.

At the end of a year Mr. Lincoln built a cabin for his family. At first it had no door, floor, or window. It had a rude fireplace and a loft. A bag of leaves in one corner of this loft was Abe's bed. This he reached by climbing a set of pegs driven into the wall.

There was but little furniture in this house, and it was very poor. A few three-legged slab stools served for chairs. There were a puncheon table and a few pewter dishes. A puncheon was made by cutting a log lengthwise into thick boards.

LINCOLN'S INDIANA HOME.

A bed was made by sticking poles into the cracks in the wall. The outer corner was held up by a forked stick. Across this frame, skins and leaves were thrown for bedding.

Life was not easy in this poor cabin in the midst of the forest. Everything that was used in the household had to be made at home.

There were no stores from which to buy, and if there had been, Thomas Lincoln had no money. How could the family get all that they needed to eat and to wear?

First they must clear out a little space in the forest, where they might plant corn. Great trees must be cut down and the underbrush cleared away.

Sometimes trees were "deadened" and left standing for a time. This means that they were killed by cutting or burning the bark around them.

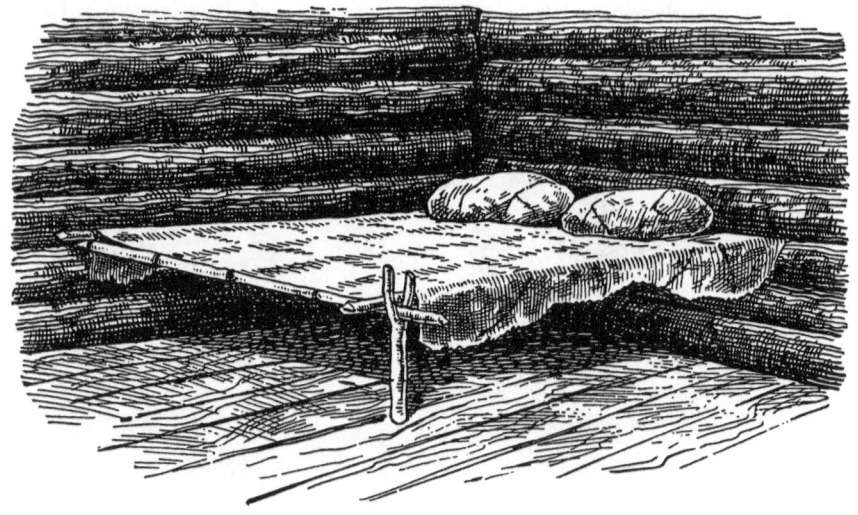

A HOME-MADE BED.

Then the sun could shine down upon the earth and make the corn grow. From the corn, meal was made and used for bread.

They raised potatoes and perhaps a few other things. For their meat, deer or turkey or other wild game was always at hand. Abe himself shot a turkey when he was only eight years old.

When a deer was killed it furnished clothing as well as food. Deerskin clothing was often worn at this time.

When they had any cloth it must be homemade. The flax, wool, or cotton was raised and prepared by the family. It was colored, spun, woven, and made into garments at home.

You can see how hard these people must have worked, to do these things. In all such work, Abraham and his sister always took part.

At this time the forests were thick and the ground was very damp, which caused much illness among the people. Mrs. Lincoln became very ill and soon died. Poor lonely little children! Their life had been hard before, but now they had no mother to care for them. They passed a dreary winter in their cheerless little cabin.

COTTON.

V. A BETTER HOME.

In about a year Mr. Lincoln went away on a journey. In a short time he came back bringing with him a stepmother for his children. She had her own three children with her, also.

FLAX.

She came in a two-horse wagon and brought furniture such as Abe and his little sister had never seen. She had a bureau worth fifty dollars, a table, real chairs, and a feather bed.

There was soon a great change in the lives of the lonely little children. Their new mother gave them good warm clothes, and they had real beds to sleep on.

She soon asked Mr. Lincoln to put down a floor in the cabin. Doors and windows were made, and it became a snug little house.

VI. LINCOLN AT SCHOOL.

So much work had to be done that there was little chance for the children to go to school. The schools, when there were any, were often far away. The best of them were very poor indeed. The teachers knew little and had only a few books.

Abe went to school whenever it was possible, and learned very fast. He became such a good speller that none could beat him in the spelling matches.

He had no slate or paper upon which to work his problems, so he made figures with a piece of charcoal on a wooden shovel.

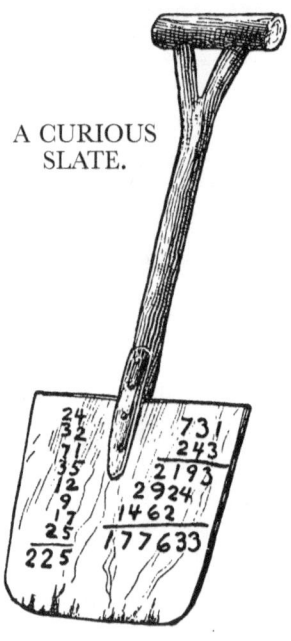

A CURIOUS SLATE.

When it was covered, he planed them off, and began again.

How he liked to read! He read over and over again every book he could get. He seemed able to remember almost everything he had read.

Though there was but little time to read or study, he used in that way what few minutes he could get. He carried his book to the field, that he might read while he was resting. He would often read until very late at night.

If there happened to be no work at home he was hired out to the neighbors for twenty-five cents a day, and the money was paid to his father.

VII. LINCOLN A YOUNG MAN.

Now you can see how Abraham spent his boyhood. He did all kinds of hard work about the farm. He cut down trees and split rails. He helped to plough and plant, to gather the crops and go to mill. He helped even in the work about the house.

But amid all this work, he found time to study and to read.

He liked to make speeches and tell stories; and all who listened to him, liked to hear him. He grew up to be the tallest and strongest young man in the neighborhood. He was perhaps also the kindest and gentlest.

When he was about twenty-one years old, his father decided to move to Illinois. Abraham went with him. He helped build the new cabin, and cut the rails to fence the land.

As soon as this work was over, the young man started out for himself.

He had not been to school more than a year. He had no money, and wore very poor clothes. He was tall and rather awkward looking.

Does he not seem a long way from the highest place in our land? And yet, you know that he finally held that place. How he did all this you will learn by and by.

ABRAHAM LINCOLN, 1858.

When we think of him and of how much he did, I am sure we feel that it is worth while to do our best—even though we are very poor.

XI. An Old Settler's Story.

I. LOST IN THE WOODS.

ONE BRIGHT AUTUMN day, several pioneers were travelling through the wilderness. One of them thus writes of the journey:—

"The driver of our ox-team told us to look at the cabin we were passing, as it was the last one we should see for forty miles. That was not a pleasant idea to the younger members of our family. Father and mother seemed to care but little, for they were used to the hardships of the wilderness.

"Slowly we passed along the narrow road. The forest was beautiful with its many bright colors. I was so pleased, that I forgot to watch the sheep that had been left in my care for a short time. Before I was aware of it, every one of them was lost in the woods.

"John and I started out to look for them. I was so anxious to find them, that I wandered too far into the woods. I soon saw that I was lost, myself. Horrible thought! I, all alone in the great forest full of wild beasts and Indians!

"I could hear my heart beat and my eyes became dim. There was no beauty in the woods to me now. I ran and hallooed till I was hoarse, but could hear no answer.

"You, who live near many people, can hardly think how it would seem to be lost in a trackless forest.

"After a few hours, I was found and brought back to the road. We had to leave our sheep to the mercy of the wolves, and proceed on our journey.

DRIVING SHEEP.

II.

"At night we camped by the side of the road. The rain came down in torrents, and the wind roared dismally in the tree-tops.

"Next morning the men went out into the woods for the oxen and other cattle. My little brother followed them, but was told to go back to the camp. He started, but went in a wrong direction.

"Just as we were ready to go on, we missed him. How frightened we were, when we knew he was lost! We called and called, till the woods echoed his name for miles around.

"At last we found him, hidden under some underbrush. He had heard us call, but thought we were Indians. So he would not answer or let himself be seen, until he was sure we were friends.

III.

"We soon started again on our journey. At noon we came to a camp fire, which had hardly burned out. It was plain that some other travellers had just passed here.

"They had killed and cooked a deer. Having eaten what they needed, they had turned the other side of it to the fire to cook, thinking perhaps somebody might come that way who would be hungry.

"We were the lucky people who found the dinner in the forest ready cooked for us. How we enjoyed the feast! We wished that we could thank our unknown friends, who had done us this kindness. Perhaps they were as happy in doing it as we were in receiving it.

"As we went on, we soon began to feel the need of water. We searched on both sides of the road for a spring, but none could be found.

"There was no water, except the black puddles in the horse tracks and wagon ruts. I became so very thirsty that at last I shut my eyes and drank from this water in the roads.

"It was not until the next day that we were made happy by reaching a sparkling stream.

"Later we passed an Indian village, which was empty at the time. Many wigwams of poles and bark were to be seen, but the owners had gone off hunting. At the close of another day we reached the end of our journey."

XII. A Story of Early Times.

I. LEAVING THE OLD HOME.

WHEN I WAS quite a small boy, my father moved from Kentucky to the central part of Indiana. His friends had said all that they could to keep him from doing such a rash thing.

They told him that the lives of all the family would be in danger, and that Indians would never let them reach the new country.

But father had made up his mind to make his home in the new "capital in the woods," and nothing could change him.

We parted sadly from our dear friends, who shed many tears as they prayed that we might be kept safe from the wild Indians.

All the furniture that we could possibly do without had been sold, and the rest, with provision for the winter, was put into a large six-horse wagon. Beds and bedding, with most of the clothing, were carried on the backs of the horses.

The feather beds were placed on the horses in such a way as to make a good platform, upon which my sister and I rode. On the first day, as we were going downhill, one horse stumbled, and we landed on the rocky road, with the beds on top of us.

We reached the Ohio River in about four days. We were ferried over in the skiff, but the horses swam across. The only way to get the wagon across was to take it to pieces and carry it over in a skiff, part at a time.

The ferryman was a white man who had lived most of his life among the Indians, having been captured by them when a child. He dressed like them, and wore rings in his nose and ears. He spoke their language and lived in a hut without table, bed, or chair.

II. INDIANS.

As we went on our journey, we had to cut away the trees so that the wagon could get through. At night some of the men watched: while the others slept. We felt very thankful each morning to find ourselves still safe from the Indians.

In about three weeks we reached the new home. Here for

"I DID NOT LOOK BACK."

the first time I saw a real Indian. I had gone to the river with the teamster to help water the horses, and had been stopped by a stranger to answer a few questions. The teamster had gone back to the wagon. I started to follow when suddenly I met a "big Injun."

I did not stop to ask him any questions or to tell him how warlike he looked. I made about as quick time to the wagon as possible. I did not look back to see what became of the Indian.

A friend in this new town to which we had come, offered at first to share his cabin with us, till we could build one of our own. Then he thought of a still better plan for us.

A man who had raised and covered a cabin had gone back for his family. He had cut no door or window or place for a chimney. Still our friend thought we might use the cabin until we could build one.

My father did not wish to cut places for the door and window, fearing he might not put them where the owner wished. So he pried up two corners of the cabin and took out the third log from the bottom so that we could climb in and out.

My grandmother was a very short, stout old lady, and it caused a great deal of fun to see her climb in and out of this cabin. No one enjoyed the fun more than the dear old lady herself.

A few boards were taken from the middle of the roof to let the smoke out. The fire was built in the centre of the room on the ground which served as the floor.

My mother lined the inside of the walls by hanging up rag carpets. This made the house quite comfortable for the short time we lived in it.

The men of the settlement helped my father build his cabin, and in a few days it was ready for use.

The fireplace was large enough to take in a back-log eight feet long, and a fore-stick ten feet in length. There were two doors on opposite sides of the house. They were placed in this way so that the fires might be built more easily.

GRANDFATHER'S LOG CABIN.

One end of a log was placed on a kind of sled called a "lizzard," to which a horse was hitched. He was driven through the house till the log was opposite the fireplace. Then it was rolled into the fire, and the horse went out through the other door. Two large logs would last a day and a night.

III. THE WINTER.

The first winter in our new home was a very cold one. The ground was covered with snow from the middle of November till March. Yet the settlers seemed contented and had many happy times.

I remember that the wild turkey we had for our Christmas dinner was killed within a few yards of our door. It was hung in front of the great fireplace by a small rope fastened to the top of the cabin. A pan was put under it to hold the gravy. The heat of the fire kept the turkey turning all the time, so that it was well cooked. What a feast it made!

In the spring my father opened a sugar camp. We had been making sugar about two weeks, when the Indians came and claimed the right to the camp. They told my father to "puc-a-chee," which meant "clear out." He did so at once.

One day my father and I were walking by the river. When near the cabin of a settler we heard a woman calling, "Help! Murder!"

We ran as fast as we could to find out what was the matter. An Indian named "Big Bottle" had come to the opposite bank of the river and commanded the woman to bring over the canoe for him.

She would not do this, so he plunged into the river, and swam across. When we came up he was running toward her cabin with his tomahawk in his hand.

As soon as he saw the white men, who rushed to her aid, he stopped and said he only meant to "scare white squaw." He was taken to his own side of the river, and told that if he tried to "scare white squaw" again, her husband would kill him.

This made him angry, and he took out his scalping knife, pointing first to her head, and then to his belt, as if he meant to take her scalp.

For some time the settlers did not feel secure from the Indians, and were easily alarmed by them.

IV. THE FOUNDING OF INDIANAPOLIS.

On the north side of our town, there were about a hundred acres of timber which had been killed by the caterpillars. All the settlers worked together and cleared out the undergrowth. This was called the "big field" and each settler had his share. It was planted with corn and pumpkins.

A fence of brush was made on the side next the town. That was all that was needed, as there was no stock likely to come into it from any other side. Besides this field shared by all, each settler had a "truck patch" of his own near his cabin.

During the first summer, there was much illness among the people. At one time, there was hardly a man well enough to hand another a drink of water.

By fall the people were well again, and all began getting ready for a great sale of lots which was to occur in October.

For days before the sale, people began coming by twos and threes, and even by dozens. There seemed to be people of all kinds and from every direction. Many brought their own provision and camped out. Some slept under trees, using their saddles for pillows.

So many people came, that it seemed as if all outdoors could hardly hold them. All were waiting for a chance to make their fortunes by buying lots in the new "capital in the woods."

The sale lasted one week, and no trouble of any kind occurred. Many people carried gold and silver money which they left in leather bags wherever they could find shelter. Yet there was no robbery, and there seemed to be no fear of any. Though they were strangers, yet they treated one another as friends.

And so ended my first year in Indianapolis. What changes have come since then can be seen by any one who walks the streets of that beautiful and prosperous city.

XIII. Grandfather's Story.

I. THE TRIP DOWN THE RIVER.

WHEN I WAS a very small boy I lived on a small rocky farm in Pennsylvania. My father had a large family of seven children to support.

He thought he could do better by going West, so he traded his farm for a flat-boat, in which we were to go down the beautiful Ohio River.

ON THE SAND BAR.

I was about five years old, and had scarcely ever been away from our farm before. I was wild with joy when we started, and could not understand why the grown folks looked sad. I well remember the tears that fell from grandma's eyes, as she handed baby Betty to my mother when we left the old home.

It seemed to me that we were going into a new world. I did not know that it was a hard, lonely life we were beginning. Of course, the grown folks knew all this. No wonder grandmother's tears fell fast. She could not hope to see us again, and she never did.

Our boat was like a house on the water. There was another family of several children with us, and of course no lack of fun among so many little ones.

How beautiful it was as we drifted slowly down the river! It was in the fall of the year and the trees looked like great bouquets. All day the boat moved slowly down the stream, but it was fastened to the shore at night.

THE STREET FULL OF STUMPS.

Once our boat ran into a sand-bar, and it took the men several days to get it off. We children were just as happy in the woods as on the boat.

We saw many Indians here, but they were friendly and did not wish to hurt us. They would look at our baby and say, "White pappoose: squaw or warrior?" Mother was afraid they would steal it, but she need not have feared. They did not admire a little weak, white baby.

II. THE JOURNEY TO THE NEW HOME.

After six weeks on the river, we landed at a little town which had a store and a blacksmith's shop. Its one street was full of stumps.

Father agreed to trade his boat for some land near the centre of the state. He and another man tramped off through the woods to build a cabin for us. We lived in the boat while they were gone.

After a while he came back for us and we started again on our journey—but this time on foot. We secured an ox-team and cart to take our goods to the new home.

The weather had grown quite cold by this time, so cold that often I had to run to keep warm. At night we built a great log fire near our camp. One night it was so cold that mother sat up all night near the fire, holding the baby on her lap to keep it from freezing.

Often we had to cut down trees to make a way for our wagon through the woods. As we travelled, we saw and heard many wild animals.

All night we could hear the howling of the wolves, but we

did not fear them because they were afraid of the log fire we kept burning near us.

In the day we could see plenty of deer, turkeys, and squirrels. We could have any of these for our dinner that we chose.

At last we reached our rude log-cabin home, and began our life in the new country.

It took us six days to make the journey. You could go as far as that to-day in two hours.

III. FOOD.

There was little that you would call comfortable in our cabin. We had but one beautiful thing, and that was the open fire. The fireplace was so large that we could burn great logs in it. As they crackled and burned they filled our rude home with rosy light.

Of course, all our food was cooked by this open fire. Over it swung a great iron crane, on which kettles could be hung. Mother had a big iron skillet with legs and a heavy lid. She baked bread in this by placing coals on the lid and under the skillet.

Sometimes she made a "Johnny cake," which was corn bread baked on a board. It was set up before the fire until one side was done, and then it was turned to let the other side bake.

I have never since tasted food that seemed so good as that cooked before the fire.

We were always sure of having plenty of meat—deer, turkey, bear, or squirrel. The trouble was to get bread. Of course, our bread was made of corn meal, and we were glad to get that.

THE OLD FIREPLACE.

We had brought some corn with us which we hoped would last till we could raise more. Corn is usually ground to make meal, but there was no mill near us at first, so we had to pound it. A mortar was made by burning out a stump, and the corn was crushed in it by a heavy weight.

Before the corn became too hard it could be grated. A piece of tin was punched full of holes, and then bent and fastened to a board. On this grater a coarse kind of meal was made which was used for mush or corn bread.

We thought ourselves well off if we had plenty of corn bread or hominy and meat.

We early settlers were always so happy to see visitors that any stranger was welcome to come to our house and stay as long as he wished.

When a new family came to live near us, all the settlers in the region helped them build their cabin. We did all we could for them, and shared everything we had with them.

POUNDING THE CORN.

IV. CLEARING LAND AND RAISING CORN.

Although it was winter when we reached our new home, there was plenty of work to do. Land must be cleared that we might raise some corn and a few vegetables the next year.

All day long the axes of my father and big brothers could be heard, chopping down the trees. Even I could help a little. I could pick up and pile the brush. Often father's axe would still be swinging far into the night, as he worked by the light of the moon.

FATHER WORKING LATE.

Of all the work in the forest, nothing pleased me so much as burning the brush. How the flames crackled and shone! Great clouds of smoke rose up amidst the trees still standing. We seemed to be getting along very fast when the brush burned up so rapidly.

After a while we had a "log rolling," with which the neighbors came to help. The logs were rolled into a great heap and burned. A "log rolling" was a kind of party. Everybody came from far and near. While the men were rolling the logs, the women were cooking, for we always had a great feast and a merry time after our work.

When spring came, father had cleared enough land for a cornfield and a "truck patch" or garden. This land could not be ploughed very easily, for it was so full of roots. One person could hardly drive the horse and hold the plough.

Although I was still very young I often sat upon old Billy's back and drove, while father held the plough. You may think that was great fun, but when the plough struck a root, and the hames struck me, I thought it was pretty hard.

When the ground was ready I helped drop the corn and father covered it with a hoe. As soon as the corn began to come up, there was work for all the children. We must get up at daylight and watch the corn all day to keep away the squirrels and crows.

They would pull up the young corn to get the little grain at the end of the sprout. How they knew the little grain was still to be found in the ground, I cannot tell; but they surely did.

The only way we had to keep them off was by running and making as much noise as we could. We would beat on old tin pans, and halloo at the top of our voices. My good dog Rover aided me much with his barking. Several years later I owned a shot-gun and this served my purpose better.

After the grain in the ground was gone, the watching was over for a time. When the new grains began to grow on the cob, war began once more. The crows again came for the corn, and we children had to frighten them away. You see now how people came to have a "scare crow" in the field.

A SCARECROW.

The mosquitoes that came about the cornfield at this time were very annoying to us. We had to build fires to keep them away.

As you may believe, this work in the cornfield was neither easy nor pleasant for us, but how glad we were when the "roasting ears" came! Perhaps we enjoyed them all the more, because we had worked so hard to protect them.

V. AFTER THE HARVEST.

After our corn was ripe and gathered in, we had another kind of party called a "corn husking." All the neighbors for miles around were invited to help. Great was the frolic and great the fun at such times.

The men and boys were divided into "sides" with captains at the head. Each side worked with might and main to husk more corn than the other side.

The captain of the winning side was often carried about on the shoulders of his men, amid great shouting from the winners.

After the work was done there was a big supper, which the women had made ready. You see we had our fun and frolics along with our work, and we enjoyed them very much.

After the corn was husked it must be shelled. This was the work for evenings and rainy days. A big coverlet was laid upon the floor, and all hands that were able shelled corn. Often, when a child, have I raised a blister on my thumb at such work!

Some of the cobs were thrown into the fire and they kept up a bright blaze. The little children had great fun making cob houses while the larger ones worked.

When a grist of corn was ready, it must be taken to the mill. A sack of corn was thrown over the horse's back. The same amount must be put into each end of the sack, or by and by it would slip off the horse.

MAKING COB HOUSES.

The nearest mill was several miles away. Many times I have gone there and waited my turn to have our corn ground. There were always a great many men and boys about the mill, waiting for their grists. Sometimes we had to wait two or three days.

"Going to the mill" was a great pleasure to me. I liked the long rides through the woods. I liked to talk with other boys and to hear the men tell stories.

You know that we did not see much company in our backwoods home. The little trip to the mill meant as much to me as a long journey would to you.

Once I was coming home from mill late at night. I was alone in the darkness of a thick forest, more than a mile from any cabin.

GOING TO THE MILL.

Suddenly I heard a great howling of wolves. Very soon I came upon a pack of them snarling over a deer they had caught. What could I do! My only pathway was blocked by a number of hungry wolves!

At first I stood still in terror. Then I left the path and felt my way through the thick brush-wood on one side as quickly and silently as I could, and so reached my home in safety.

Grandfather's Story

We lived in our new home a number of years before we had any wheat. At last father raised a small patch, which was cut with a sickle and bound into bundles by hand.

There were no such things as reapers and self-binders in those days. When thrashing time came, the wheat stalks were spread out and pounded with a heavy flail, till the grains rattled out. Then the straws were gathered up and taken away.

FANNING AWAY THE CHAFF.

The wheat and chaff were thrown up into the air while two men fanned away the chaff with a sheet, and the wheat fell to the ground. Sometimes, instead of using a flail, horses were driven over the wheat to thrash out the grain.

We felt rich when we were able to have a little wheat bread! We thought it so fine that we called it "cake."

VI. SCHOOLS.

I wish that I could let my little friends peep into the schoolhouse of my "boy days." Two miles from our home was a little log cabin that had once been used as a dwelling, but was now our schoolhouse. We followed a "blazed" path through the forest to reach it.

THE BLAZED PATH THROUGH THE WOODS.

This means that little pieces of bark had been cut off some of the trees along our way. When we saw such a mark in a tree we went toward it. Then we looked for the next tree that was "blazed," and so on. In this way we were guided to our schoolhouse.

What an odd little house it would seem to you! It had a stick chimney, clapboard roof, a greased paper window, and puncheon floor. Inside, the seats were placed around three sides of the room. The fireplace was in the fourth side.

The teacher, or "master," as we called him, sat in the middle of the room. On one side of the room was a kind of shelf made of a puncheon, and high enough to write upon. In front of this was a bench made also of a puncheon. This was the seat for the big scholars. When they wished to write they turned their backs toward the teacher and wrote upon the shelf.

On two sides of the room were benches made for the little children. They did not need any desk. Of course, they could not write! They must study their books all day long. The only rest from their study was at the time the "master" called them up to "say their lessons."

What do you suppose their first book was—a pretty pictured reader like yours? No indeed; it was a spelling book. Each little child must begin by learning his "a-b-c's"! I had not even a book from which to learn these at first. One of my big brothers made the letters on a board. For a long time I carried this to school to study.

After we had learned our letters we must learn to spell "bā, bē, bī, bō, bū," and so on. Next we learned to spell little words, then big words and bigger words. After that we might begin to read very little sentences. We had no drawing or writing or sewing or letters or pretty things to use at our seats. We had to study our books.

Do you wonder that it was a long time before we learned to read in such a school? It was much longer before we learned to write or "cipher." But we could spell—that was the chief thing.

We had what was called a "loud school." The "master" would say, "Study your spelling lessons." Then every child in the school would take his book and shout, "l-a la, d-y dy, lady; s-h-a sha, d-y dy, shady," and so on all through his lesson. Think, if you can, what a noise that would make.

If the noise grew too great, the master would rap on his desk with a ruler and say, "Silence!" Then the noise would become a little less for a time.

Is it strange that the boys and girls sometimes grew very tired in this school? I do not wonder that the master kept in sight a number of large switches. He used them very often to make the children attend to their work.

Still we had some pleasant times, too, in going to these schools. There was the long walk through the beautiful woods. We learned many things there of animals and birds and flowers that you have never seen. Then what good times we had in being with other children!

Ah! what fun we had at recess! We had no little gravel-covered yard where we dared not run for fear of knocking some one down. Instead of that, there were the big woods in which we might run and play. We could go where we liked, if we did not get too far away to hear the master call, "Books!" That was his way of ringing the recess bell.

Then there were the long noons every day! Of course, we all brought our dinners, as it was too far to go home. When it was pleasant weather we could eat in the woods.

Such fun as we had playing games! Little girls played "King William," "Blackman," "Hide and Seek," and other games. The old trees made the best of hiding places.

THE BEST HIDING PLACE.

The boys, of course, took more pleasure in playing ball, climbing trees, jumping, racing, and so on.

Our school lasted only a few months in the year. We could not always go, even when the school was open. The big boys and girls must stay at home when there was work to do. They could go only on rainy days, or when there was no work.

Sometimes there was a school for a few weeks in summer. Only the little children went then, for, of course, this was the time when all the big ones had to work hard.

A woman taught this school. People thought a woman could not teach big boys, because she was not strong enough to "thrash" them.

I fear that many of the children learned but little in our old-time schools. The bright ones would learn pretty fast, as the master heard them say their lessons as often as they wished. The slow ones learned almost nothing.

Often children would go to school all that they could for several years and not be able to read as well as you can after going one year. Perhaps they would have to leave school and go to work when they had not learned enough to be able to read a story or write a letter.

VII. CLOTHING.

You have seen how we got our food in our pioneer homes. We also provided our clothes by our own work. In the earliest times much clothing was made of deerskin. Later, we made cloth of wool, when we were able to protect our sheep from the wolves.

SHEARING SHEEP.

We children watched the making of our clothes from the time the wool was cut from the sheep till the garments were ready to wear.

Father washed the sheep and cut off the wool. Mother carded and spun it, then wove and colored it, and made it into clothes for us.

Our summer clothing was made from flax. This we raised ourselves and obtained a kind of thread from its stem. There were many parts of the work in which we children could help.

Our shoes, like our clothes, were made at home. At first father made them for his own family. In later times a shoemaker travelled from house to house, making shoes for us all.

It was very hard to provide shoes for all the family. Often the little children went barefooted. They had to stay in the house in very cold weather. Many grown people also had no shoes.

Would it not seem queer to see a young lady walk to church barefooted? I have often seen that. She carried her shoes with her, stopping just before she reached the church to put them on. That was a good plan, especially if there was a stream to wade on the way. It was a good way to save shoes, too.

We knew how hard it was to get our clothes, so we took good care of them. They were not so fine or so pretty as yours, but they were warm and comfortable, and we were satisfied with them.

VIII. LACK OF CONVENIENCES.

You have many things in your houses that we had not. Perhaps you can hardly see how we did without them. What do you think you would do if you had no matches? I never saw a match when I was a child.

We did not often let the fire in the big fireplace go out. At night we covered up the coals with ashes. In the morning the live coals were raked out and more wood was put on.

If the fire went out, we would go to the nearest neighbor, perhaps a mile away, to "borrow fire." This means that we brought home a few live coals covered with ashes.

There was another way of starting a fire. We had a kind of hard stone called flint. When we struck it with a piece of steel, the sparks flew. We let these fall on a bunch of tow, which would burn readily. This would start the punk with which we kindled a fire.

We had no gas or lamps, and when I can first remember, not even candles to light our houses. The light from the fireplace was usually all we needed. We had a kind of lamp that looked like a dish with a rag in it; in this we burned melted lard.

Sometimes a turnip was scraped out and used to hold the lard. Was not that a queer lamp? It gave about as much light as a match. Later we made candles and thought them very fine.

In the early days we told the time of day by the sun, for we had no clocks or watches. Often I have looked at the shadow on the floor to tell what time it was. On cloudy days, of course, we could only guess at the time.

The sun told us direction also, as well as time. At night we could tell north by the north star. If we were lost in the woods, there was another way to tell which was north. We had only to look at the trees, to see upon which side the moss grew. It grows upon the north side, for it likes the shade better than the sunshine.

IX. MONEY.

Does it seem strange to you that we rarely saw money? What use had we for money? There was little need for us to buy anything. We made our own clothes, as well as the cloth from which they were made. We got our food from the forest or from our own "truck patch." We made our own houses and what was in them.

There were at first no stores from which to buy. A little later we traded articles with other people, just as children exchange their play-things.

There were some things which people would always take in trade, such as furs. The skins of raccoons would be taken for work or goods as money is now. Four "coonskins" were equal to a dollar.

COONSKIN.

Then there were some kinds of roots that would always pass just as money will now. This was true of ginseng, which was called "sang." People spent much time digging "sang." Would it not seem queer to you to dig up money from the ground?

We had a few foreign coins. There was one called a fip, worth about six and one-fourth cents. Another, worth twelve and one-half cents, was called a bit. We had a big copper cent about the size of a silver half-dollar.

By and by we had our own American money. If we had not the right change, a piece of money was often cut into two or four pieces. It has been only a few years since I saw this cut money.

A FIP, WORTH 6¼ CENTS.   A BIT, WORTH 12½ CENTS.

These were silver coins about the size of our present 1-cent and 5-cent pieces. These drawings are somewhat larger to show the detail.

X. PIONEER PREACHERS.

Of course, there were no churches among us at first; and such a thing as a Sunday school was not thought of. We had our meetings in some cabin, or out under the trees. Later we had our little log churches built like the houses.

Sometimes a travelling preacher visited us. The people would come for miles and miles to hear him preach.

The preacher was a hunter and a pioneer like the rest of us. It was no easy task for him to go about from place to place, through the thick woods and muddy swamps. Yet he was brave and cheerful, and might be heard singing hymns at the top of his voice, as he went on his lonely way.

He went on horseback and carried his rifle and blanket with him. At night he would often be far from any settlement. Then he rolled himself up in his blanket, and slept on the ground near his camp fire.

He needed his rifle to protect him from unfriendly Indians, and to kill game for food. He carried punk and flint and tow with him, that he might make a fire to cook his food.

A TRAVELLING PREACHER.

Once a preacher was going through the woods on a cold, rainy day. He had made a fire, after much trouble, and cooked his last bit of meat. Just as he sat down to eat his dinner, five

Indians appeared. The preacher saw that they looked hungry, and that they expected him to give them something to eat. He did so, and they ate it all, grunting their thanks as they walked off.

Tired, wet, and hungry, the preacher spent the rest of the day trying to find some food for himself. Just before night the Indians appeared again, saying, "White man give Indian to eat; Indian give white man to eat." They made a fire and gave him quite a feast. They took care of him that night, and gave him food to carry with him next day.

When these preachers came to any settlement they were made very welcome. Even the poorest pioneer was glad to share all he had with them. People listened to their preaching with great interest and respect.

XI. MAILS—DIFFICULTIES OF TRADE.

It was a great thing for our town when we began to get mail regularly. At first, the letters were brought twice a month by men on horseback. They carried little horns, which they blew loudly as they came into town. How the people would flock out to meet them. Everybody hoped to get a letter from some one "Back East."

The mail carriers often had to swim all the streams in their way. Sometimes they were several days behind time, on account of high water. I have often seen the postmaster spreading the mail out in the sun to dry.

CARRYING THE MAILS.

It is a very good thing for people in a new country to be able even to hear from the older states once in a while. But that is not enough. There must be some way for people to go easily from place to place. They must have some way of taking their goods to market.

In some parts of the country canals had been dug, hundreds of miles long. Boats were drawn on these by horses driven along a towpath by the side of the canal. This made a safe though a slow way of travel.

By and by, steamboats were invented, and they came regularly down the Ohio River, instead of the flat-boats of earlier times.

But we, who lived away from any large river, had a much harder time. If we had anything to sell, it was hard to take it to market. A man who had hogs to sell would walk seventy-five or

TOWING CANAL BOATS.

one hundred miles, driving them. After they were sold, he walked home again.

Not far from us was a river, down which we sometimes took our produce in a small flat-boat. We sold both the goods and the boat, and walked home. Think of the time and trouble such a trip meant.

I have sometimes carried eggs to town to sell. Each egg was wrapped by itself in a piece of tow. They were all put into a sack, which was placed on a horse's back. Of course the horse must walk all the way to keep the eggs from breaking. Perhaps it would take all day to go to the nearest store and back, just to sell a few eggs.

XII. ROADS, NEW SETTLERS, STAGES.

People soon began to feel that we must have better roads. We had a kind of road called corduroy, which was made by throwing logs down crosswise into the road. The logs kept wagons from sinking so deep into the mud that they could not get out. The wagon went with a jolt from one log to the next. That was pretty rough riding, as you may know.

These roads were afterward made into pikes which were much better for travellers. As the roads became better, new settlers began to flock into the country.

Every day numbers of moving-wagons could be seen bringing families to the new country. They came in groups, or long trains, but not often alone.

The wagons were drawn by three or four horses, and were covered with canvas or bed quilts. Furniture and feather beds were sticking out on all sides, and often little children peeped out also.

By the side of each wagon walked a sturdy man, driving the horses. Perhaps his wife walked near him, carrying a baby. Other children followed, driving the cows and sheep. At night the movers camped out like an army.

This is the way moving was done only a few years ago.

By and by there began to be regular modes of travel, by means of a stage. Four strong horses pulled this big, heavy stage. It had a regular route, and stopped at places along the road, called inns. Here people could get meals or spend the night. Here the horses were changed, and a fresh team started out.

The driver sat on top of the stage and carried a horn with him, which he blew very loudly as the stage came into town. Everybody was glad to see it come in. It was the event of the day. How interesting every traveller was! Perhaps he had come from a great distance.

The stages also carried the mails to the larger towns. The horseback riders took the mail only to such towns as the stage did not visit.

XIII. CARS—TELEGRAPH.

Little by little our life in the new country began to change. As we could travel about better, it was easier to sell what we raised and to buy what we needed. We no longer had to make everything for ourselves. In this way we had less work to do at home.

One day we heard of the wonderful steam cars. We were told they could go ten miles an hour. People said they ran so smoothly that we could not only read but we could write in them!

Before long a railroad was commenced in our own state. It took a long time to build it, but at last the road reached the town near us. On a certain day the great steam horse was to come into that town for the first time. What a great day it was!

AN OLD-FASHIONED TRAIN OF CARS.

Everybody who could do so went to see the cars come in. For a long distance the track was lined with people. Even now I seem to hear the buzz of voices of the waiting crowd.

At last we could just see the engine far away in the distance. What a frightful thing it was, as it came rushing up the iron track with a great noise! It seemed like a big wild animal running away.

It was received by shouts from the crowd. A speech was made from the top of a car at the depot. There was music by the band, and the day closed with fireworks.

I well remember my first ride on the cars. It seemed as if I were in a wagon with the horses running away, and no one holding the lines.

Of course, the cars did not go so fast then as they do now. The roads were not so smooth, and the cars were not so elegant. You would think our first cars very rough and slow; but they seemed very fine and swift to us.

Several years later the telegraph first came to our town. One old settler remarked as he heard the message read, "Well, John, old Jerry has lived to see the day when a streak of lightning can be made to run along a clothesline, just like some wild animal along a worm fence, and carry news from one end of the earth to the other!"

And now we were no longer alone in the back-woods. We could hear in a few minutes what was happening all over the world. We could readily send our goods to market. We could get money for them, and buy goods that came from far away.

We could go back to our old homes in the East more easily than we could travel twenty miles when we first came.

The coming of the cars and telegraph brought rapid changes to our new country. Now we can have nearly the same pleasures and advantages that people have in the older states.

You could not have had all these good things, had some one not lived here before you, who worked hard and did without much which you think necessary. Do not forget this, when you see the white-haired pioneers who are still here.

The brave, true lives of these hardy men and women have made this beautiful country possible. There is no better thing to do than to live so that other people will be happier because of your life.

www.ingramcontent.com/pod-product-compliance
Lightning Source LLC
LaVergne TN
LVHW041854070526
838199LV00045BB/1593